DATE DUE

JAN 3 1999			
NOV 1 0 2000			
OCT 0 7 2003			
NOV 1 7 2003			
DEC 2 2 2003			
MAY 1 3 2004			
NOV 2 6 2007			
GAYLORD			PRINTED IN U.S.A.

The Wonder of
WHALES

Adapted from Tom Wolpert's *Whale Magic for Kids*
by Valerie Weber
Photography by Flip Nicklin

Gareth Stevens Publishing
MILWAUKEE

8-14-97

For a free color catalog describing Gareth Stevens' list of high-quality books, call 1-800-341-3569 (USA) or 1-800-461-9120 (Canada).

Library of Congress Cataloging-in-Publication Data

Weber, Valerie.
    The wonder of whales / adapted from Tom Wolpert's Whale magic for kids by Valerie Weber ; photography by
Flip Nicklin.
        p. cm. — (Animal wonders)
    Includes index.
    Summary: Text and photographs introduce Earth's largest living creature, the whale.
    ISBN 0-8368-0857-6
    1. Whales—Juvenile literature. [1. Whales.] I. Nicklin, Flip, ill. II. Wolpert, Tom. Whale magic for kids. III.
Title. IV. Series.
    QL737.C4W39   1992
    599.5—dc20   92-16946

North American edition first published in 1992 by
Gareth Stevens Publishing
1555 North RiverCenter Drive, Suite 201
Milwaukee, WI 53212, USA

This U.S. edition is abridged from *Whale Magic for Kids,* copyright © 1990 by NorthWord Press, Inc., and
written by Tom Wolpert, first published in 1990 by NorthWord Press, Inc., and published in a library
edition by Gareth Stevens, Inc. Additional end matter copyright © 1992 by Gareth Stevens, Inc.

Cover design: Kristi Ludwig

Printed in the United States of America

   3 4 5 6 7 8 9 98 97 96 95

Whales swim the seas all over the world.

They may look like fish, but they are *mammals*, like us.

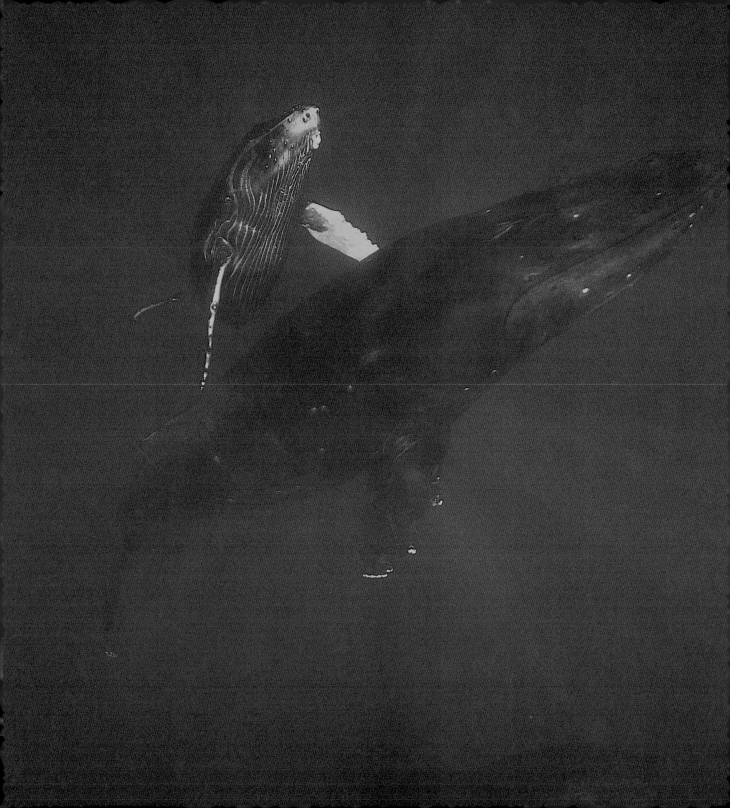

Like all mammals, whales give birth to live young and *nurse* their babies.

Like people and other mammals, whales also breathe through lungs, not through gills like fish. But unlike people, whales cannot smell. They also don't have ears — just tiny ear openings at the sides of their head.

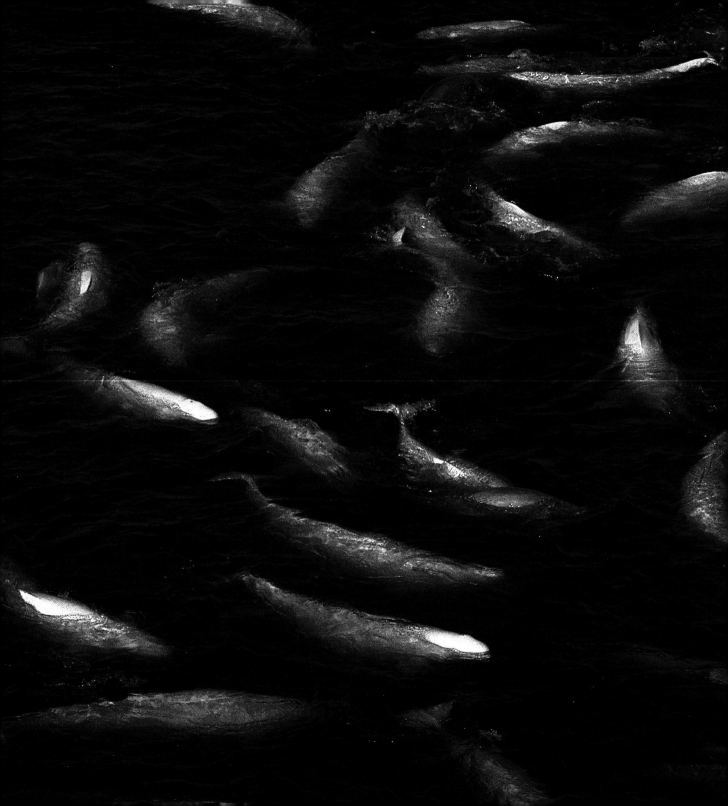

Some whales travel in large groups called *pods*. Others swim in family groups with just two or three whales.

A female whale is called a cow, and her baby is a calf.

A cow keeps her calf near her and helps it swim.

Two front flippers help
guide the whale through the
water, while its powerful
tail pushes it along.

Whales protect calves with all their strength and size.

As far as we know, whales don't normally fight among themselves. And they do not attack humans or boats.

Besides people, whales have only one other *predator*. Killer whales, like those resting here, attack and eat baby whales.

A whale takes deep breaths of air before diving deep to feed. When it comes to the surface, it *exhales* through its *blowhole*. Its hot breath turns into fog when it meets the cold air.

Whales were once hunted by *whalers* following these spurts of fog. In fact, at one time, people killed so many whales that they were in danger of becoming *extinct*. Now, most countries have laws that try to stop people from hunting these giants of the deep.

Long ago, whales *evolved* from mammals that lived on land. These creatures found that food was very plentiful in the water, so they fed in the seas more and more. It took millions of years, but to make feeding in the sea easier, their bodies gradually took the shape of fish.

It's hard to imagine that whales are still related to

a land mammal like the hippopotamus!

Whales are divided into two groups: *toothed* and *baleen*.

Toothed whales eat fish and squid whole.

The sperm whale (shown above) is the largest toothed whale.

A long spiral tusk juts out of the male narwhal whale (left). He sometimes fights other narwhals with it to show which is the strongest.

This baby beluga whale clings to its mother's back as she swims. Sometimes, the young beluga may join other youngsters in a nursery guarded by mothers. The color of the baby's skin will change as the beluga grows older.

Killer whales leap with power and grace.

They can travel as fast as a car on a city street!

The second group of whales is called baleen whales.

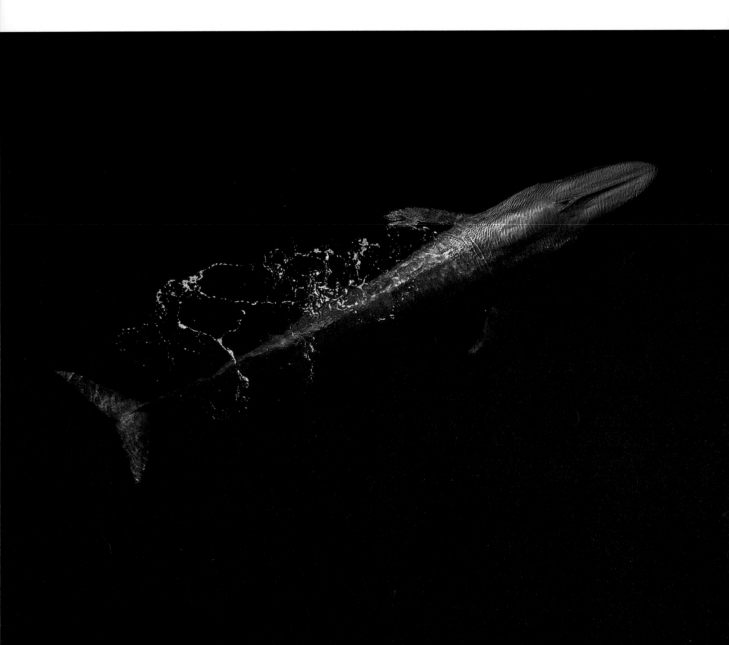

A baleen whale, like the blue whale shown here, gulps seawater or mud from the ocean floor. This contains millions of tiny plants and animals — whale food. Then, the whale squeezes the mud or water through rows of plates in its mouth called baleen. Only the food is left behind.

The humpback whale is also a baleen whale. It gets its name from the roll of fat that forms a hump on its back. Other animals, like *barnacles* and *crustaceans*, attach themselves to the humpback's skin. You can see them on the whale's flipper on the previous page.

The right whale skims the ocean surface for tiny plants and animals.

The huge right whale got
its name because it was the
"right" whale for whalers to
kill.   Its body could be
made into many products.
It also moves slowly and
floats when it's killed.

Now the right whale is an *endangered species*. No one is allowed to hunt it.

Today, we know more about whales than ever before. We have begun to cherish them, not for the products we can turn them into, but for the beauty and mystery they give our world.

Glossary

baleen — a hard substance found in two rows of plates attached to the top jaw of a whale

barnacle — a small sea animal with a hard shell that attaches itself to boat bottoms, under-sea rocks, and whales

blowhole — a nostril on the top of the whale's head

crustaceans — a group of animals that live mostly in water and have hard outer coverings

endangered species — a group of animals or plants that is in danger of being killed off completely

evolve — to develop gradually from something else

exhale — to breathe out

extinct — no longer existing in a live form

mammals — warm-blooded animals that give birth to their young live and nurse them with milk from their own bodies; mammals usually have some hair or fur on their bodies

nurse — to feed a baby milk from its mother's breast

pod — a number of animals collected together

predator — an animal that lives by eating other animals

toothed — having teeth

whaler — a person who hunts whales

Index